Risk Management

The Ultimate Guide to Risk Management for Beginners

Contents

Introduction

Plenty of people think they can beat the market. They pick high growth stocks or value stocks, they watch their portfolios carefully, and they think they'll do well. But if they don't know about risk management, they could come a cropper. Read investment sites aimed at retail investors and you will almost never come across the concept of risk management.

Many small and medium-sized businesses don't have a risk manager. They have a health and safety officer. They have a finance director. But without a risk manager, there's no one to bring the different strands of risk together and assess exactly how much risk the business can - and should - take on board, or to measure the risk it's actually taking.

Risk management is a discipline that's been applied most strictly in the banking sector, largely as a result of a series of trading scandals and bank failures during the 1990s and the first decade of the 21st century. There have been flash crashes and liquidity squeezes, 'fat fingers' and all kinds of bubbles, and although we may not have done with boom and bust, a lot of people are trying to make sure that their extremes are more tightly managed than used to be the case.

In a major investment bank the risk management function may be very highly resourced and carry out calculations of quite staggering complexity. The authorities have made major moves in enforcing good risk management discipline - the Sarbanes-Oxley Act (2002), Basel II (2004) and now Basel III have all helped to establish RM and standardize basic RM principles across the banking industry.

But the basic concepts of risk management are useful to the individual investor or the small business owner. In this book, we might not go into the advanced details of how to calculate the Black-Scholes formula or run a global banking RM function, but we'll show you how thinking about risk in an educated way can transform your investment and business prospects.

Chapter 1 – The Benefits of Risk Management

What comes into your mind when you hear the word 'risk'? Do you automatically feel threatened - 'at risk' of something nasty happening? Or do you feel fired up to go and take a risk?

Well hold your horses, because I didn't quantify that risk. 'Risk' might mean the currently very slow erosion of the value of a cash holding by inflation - if you don't find a better investment than cash within ten years, you could lose 10% of the spending power of your capital. Or it might mean buying a stock that will triple in price if the company doesn't go bust, but you might lose all your money - a very high and immediate risk.

So first of all, we need to think about how to quantify risk. That has a big benefit in taking the emotion out of the word, and it allows us to compare different courses of action as being more or less risky, rather than having a little siren go off that blares 'risk!' at some courses of action but doesn't, perhaps, consider the less obvious risks behind others.

We also need to think about human behavior. Human beings are not, in a state of nature, perfect risk managers. They tend to exhibit irrational behavior. For instance, they tend to prefer loss avoidance to profit maximization even though, in the long run, this delivers them very poor returns. They double up on losing bets and cut their winning positions, instead of the other way round. And their mathematical ability is frequently a long way short of what they need to evaluate risks properly.

Organizational behavior can also be problematic - it's not unknown for senior management to 'shoot the messenger' rather than listening to what their risk managers are telling them.

We also need to think about risk and reward. Generally, the two correlate pretty well - the higher the risk you take, the higher the reward you'll get for taking it. When that's not the case, there's something wrong. Obviously, if the market is willing to give you a high reward despite the fact you're not running much risk, that's a bet you should take (after looking very hard to see whether there's a catch). O the other hand, if a high risk doesn't seem to have a good upside, you'd turn it down immediately.

The bond market at the beginning of 2018 seems to be one of those "run-a-mile-from" opportunities; bonds offer almost zero interest yield (reward), yet the risk of prices falling if interest rates go up is very high. But some financial advisers are still pushing bond funds - including those which hold mainly long-dated bonds, most prone to capital loss if yields rise - "because bonds are safer than equities."

Remember, many investors think that property is 'safe', bonds are 'safe', and stocks are 'risky'. Yet when you quantify risk you can see that bonds and bond-proxies like utilities currently have relatively high risk and low reward, while growth stocks appear to offer a higher upside and slightly lower risk. Lazy thinking about 'safe' and 'risky' has often led professional as well as individual investors into horrible situations like the sub-prime mortgage crash or the Bernie Madoff scam. Do the numbers, think about the real level of risk, and you can protect yourself against many disasters that are waiting to happen.

In a business, risk and reward also play out within corporate strategies. For instance, many software businesses refused to transition to Software as a Service, because it would have cannibalized their existing earnings from license sales. They looked only at the risk to their existing business - not at the reward from the new strategy. In fact, although businesses which moved to a subscription model had a few choppy years, they increased their market share at the expense of other software vendors - a risk not considered by the businesses that got left behind.

You might also apply risk management techniques to assessing your sales strategy. If you sell for cash, you run no risk at all of not being paid - but you might be missing out on sales that you could gain if you allowed customers 30 days' credit. As so often, to get the right answer you'll need to do the numbers, but you also need to think about your risk appetite - what level of risk is acceptable? Are you prepared to lose ten percent of your profits, in the worst case?

You might apply RM techniques to your insurance. You might decide to cut your costs by choosing a higher excess, because you know you can afford to lose $500 on a single event, and that will save you $70 a year on insurance. On the other hand, if you don't have much in savings and you're paying a big mortgage, you might decide to pay a higher insurance bill to ensure you'll never be out of pocket. Again, you are choosing your level of risk by quantifying the risks and making a comparison.

Risk management will help you to *manage uncertainty,* and to transfer or mitigate the risks that you run, via insurance, hedging and other techniques. Obviously, your business proposition or your investment selection will be key to your returns - and we all hope to get that 100% right. But in the real world, we're never going to be right 100% of the time - there are always uncertainties and unknowables out there - so risk management aims to let you manage those risks, rather than just worry about them.

Remember that you can be correct, and still lose. John Maynard Keynes famously said that stock markets can stay irrational longer than you can remain solvent; risk management is there to stop you going bust while you're waiting for the market to return to normality (and it should also help keep you solvent if you just happen to be wrong).

Sometimes investors are absolutely right that a crash is coming - but they lose for some other reason. For instance, covered warrants gave investors a chance either to bet against the London housing market, or to use the instrument as a hedge against loss of value in their principal residences if the market fell - but many who bought covered warrants lost out because the timing of the eventual fall was later than expected, and the warrants expired before they showed a profit.

In the case of the 1985 tin price crash, the London Metals Exchange suspended trading of tin contracts, which didn't reappear for three years. Traders who shorted tin futures lost, because they couldn't trade out of their positions to take their profits. If they'd read this book, they might have protected themselves better from liquidity risk - or made sure they controlled their liabilities on the trade.

Running a business without risk management is like going to sea without a life-belt. Even if your risk management is pretty basic and back-of-envelope, and your risk management officer is the finance director after three o'clock on Friday afternoons, it's better than nothing - and once you've started looking at things from a risk perspective, you'll never see them the same way again.

Just make sure the risk tail doesn't wag the management dog. Risk management isn't about avoiding risk, it's about controlling it. If you find 'risk management' is getting used as a reason for not innovating, not entering new markets, or not considering new asset classes for an investment portfolio, chances are it's being done wrong. Risk management doesn't set your strategy - it simply looks at the risks of pursuing that strategy, quantifies that risk, and then looks at how that risk can be transferred or controlled, if it's uncomfortable with it. Enabling controlled, strategic risk taking should benefit your business or investments - and that's what RM is all about.

Chapter 2 – The basic concepts and vocabulary of risk management

Risk management depends on various basic concepts, which we'll explain in this chapter. Some are obvious - others a little less so. There's also a fair amount of vocabulary you'll need to get under your belt.

Risk exposure is your total monetary exposure to a certain risk. For instance, if you export to Japan, you will have a major risk exposure - your invoices are paid in yen and your business has dollar costs. If the exchange rate moves, you might lose out. Start by identifying and then quantifying your risk exposures - that allows you to see the major risks facing your business, and you can then decide how to address them.

Risk exposure in this case would be the same amount as your total sales to Japan. But in the case of some investments, which are geared, your risk exposure could be more than the market value of the investment.

If your exposure crystallizes, you have a *risk event*.

Any risk has two aspects, *variability* and *size*. Suppose I'm running an outdoor beer and music festival and I'm looking at all the risks that could impact my profit on the event.

- A *large* risk event is a really major weather event, like a tornado, or flooding of the site. However, the event isn't very likely (variability).

- A couple of rain showers is a *small* risk event. However, it's much more likely, and it could still deter visitors from attending, and spoil the enjoyment of those who have turned up.

These two risks can be addressed in different ways. I can probably get reasonably priced insurance against severe weather risks. Insuring against any rain at all could be prohibitively expensive - on the other hand I could hire a large marquee, and lay in some kitty litter for soaking up muddy patches or leaks. (I could also make sure the big marquee is well publicized.)

Expected value is a useful technique to use in evaluating risks. You estimate the probability of a risk event happening, and multiply the expected loss by the probability to get an *expected value*. That's a useful short-cut to ranking risks, particularly operational risks. For instance, I could consider operational risks in a small services business this way:

Risk	Probability	Lost earnings	Expected Value
Major server outage (4 hours)	4%	$1,500	$60
Destruction of business premises (lost earnings only: value of property is covered by insurance)	0.1%	$35,000	$35
Member of staff leaves: can't be replaced for a month	4%	$16,000	$640

Most businesses probably worry more about the destruction of their premises and having to work out of temporary accommodation, perhaps with a skeleton staff; but actually, losing a staff member is much worse news if you look at the expected value, because it's more likely to happen.

Standard deviation is a measure of how values spread out around the mean (average). So for instance, if we look at a representative selection of US citizens, most of them will be around 5 feet 9 inches (men) / 5 feet 4 inches (women). The further away from those heights you get, the fewer people you will see. Right at the extremes, you'll find very, very few extremely short or extremely tall people. That's a *normal distribution* (remember that not all distributions are normal, though). Plot that on a chart and it will look a bit like a tricorn hat or a python that's just eaten an elephant, or a rather flat bell - that's why it's called a *bell curve*. For each individual, we can say 'Bob is 4 feet 10 inches high', or we can express this as 'Bob is 1.2 standard deviations below the mean'. You might also look at historical stock market crashes, in terms of how severe the fall in price over a week or a month was, and in that case, you could look at 2007 and say "Wow, that was a 14 SD event" - that is, it was at the extreme end of the bell curve, of extreme severity.

$$s = \sqrt{\frac{\sum_{i=1}^{N}(x_i - \overline{x})^2}{N-1}}.$$

For reference, here's the formula for calculating a standard deviation: In risk management we look at probabilities, but we're often going to be most concerned with extreme events, because these are the ones that put the business under extreme stress. It's interesting to note the impact that events at the far end of the distribution curve can have. For instance, if you held a portfolio of stocks for 50 years, you'd find that under 100 days - one-third of one year - contributed by far the majority of your return. (Of course, it would be great if you knew in advance which days those were going to be, but that ain't the way the cookie crumbles!)

Another mathematical concept we'll need to use is the *confidence level*. A confidence level of 99% means we are 99% certain that the results would be repeated if we took a different statistical sample. For instance, you might survey how many tracks people have in their iTunes libraries. You could plot that as a distribution curve. For a 95% confidence level, you exclude the results of the top 2.5% and bottom 2.5% of the distribution - the people who have only a handful of tracks, and those who have bought everything they can see.

Volatility is a measure of the dispersion of returns - technically, the standard deviation of returns from a stock around its average return over time. Basically a stock with a lower volatility will tend not to see its price move very much - it might track upwards, but in small steps - while a high volatility stock sees wide swings in pricing. As with the term 'risk', 'volatility' is a neutral term - high volatility isn't bad in itself. Indeed, low volatility can be very bad news if it means a share price just isn't moving at all!

Disaggregating risks is a key concept in financial risk management. If you buy a bond in a foreign currency, for instance, you have a number of risks - credit risk, currency exchange risk, and interest rate risk, all tied up in one investment. But using various kinds of derivatives, or by hedging, you can strip the risks apart so that if, for instance, you've got a strong view on the credit quality of that particular company, you can 'insure away' the currency risk and interest rate risk to leave yourself purely exposed to the credit risk. (It's like being offered an auction lot with one picture you're sure is a genuine van Gogh, and a lot of others that may or may not be Rothkos. If you're a van Gogh expert, selling the rest of the pictures to another buyer at your cost price means you're backing your judgment.

Risk control is about deciding what to do with risk. You can keep it, avoid it, transfer it, or mitigate it.

- Keeping risk - you may decide that you're willing to take on higher volatility investments, because you want a higher return. Or you might take on corporate customers who represent a high risk of non-payment, because they're also fast-growing companies and you think that will help your business grow faster.

- Avoiding risk - you might decide to avoid longer-dated bonds entirely in view of the potential risk of capital loss if interest rates rise. You might decide that getting involved in a new market that is just opening up - for instance, a country where sanctions have just been lifted - represents too high a risk for your limited resources.

- Transferring risk can be done a number of ways. Insurance is one - you insure your business premises, you might take on liability or malpractice insurance. You might use a subcontractor for some business processes; you might use derivatives or hedging to offset financial exposures.

- Mitigating risk means taking action to reduce the severity of its effects. As an investor, for instance, I can set a stop loss, and make sure no single position accounts for more than 10% of my total portfolio. A lender can mitigate credit risk by taking collateral - that's how mortgages work. Operationally, a bank might mitigate the risk of 'fat finger' (traders pushing the wrong button by mistake and selling a million shares instead of just 100,000) by setting limits on the size of trades.

Me and my bandsaw

I have a bandsaw. It's a useful tool in a workshop as it can cut through wood very quickly and easily. It's also dangerous - a band of toothed steel running round at over 1,000 RPM. It's also a useful tool for showing the four different ways of dealing with risk.

- Take on the risk - I use my bandsaw and chop my wood because I want to build a bookcase, and the saw lets me do it.

- Avoid the risk - I decide I really don't like using machine tools, and I use a handsaw. It takes a lot longer but I don't care. (I would care, though, if I was selling bookcases, because hours of my time cost money - and I might not get a price that gave me a good return on my time.)

- Transfer the risk. "Hey, Joe, can you saw this wood for me?"

- Mitigate the risk. I don't want my fingers going under that blade, so I use a push-stick and I make sure the guard is adjusted to prevent my hands encountering the blade.

Above all, you need to remember the key concept behind risk management, which is that **every decision involves risk.** You may have to cross a busy road full of fast traffic to get to the store; you perceive a high risk of being run over, and no risk at all in waiting. But suppose you had to wait ten hours? Two days? A week? Over the long term, there is obviously another major risk to be considered, that of starving to death. Every investment is a risk - but keeping your money in an easy access account is also a risk, because inflation will erode the spending power of your money (remember - low risk equals low return). There is no 'risk off' option. Your job is to look at the risks and rewards of various courses of action and to find the one which delivers what you consider the optimum balance of the two.

Chapter 3 – Enterprise risk management

Often, we think of risk in terms of specific one-off decisions: buying a bond, making a loan, extending credit to a particular customer. Where Enterprise Risk Management (ERM) is different is that it looks at risk across the entire business, trying to come up with a 'risk budget' and to manage and monitor risk in the same way that the finance department budgets and monitors a business's financial situation.

You need first to think about your strategic objectives - how much risk do you want to assume? Keep the risk/reward ratio in mind as you do so. You also need to think about what areas of risk you'll take on, and what types of risk you want to transfer.

- One finance boutique decides it is willing to take on higher risks in search of higher profits. On the other hand a challenger bank lending to small and medium-sized enterprises decides that since its chosen lending area is already relatively high risk, it needs to take a conservative approach to managing its funding and treasury.

- A business that makes high specification engineering components for the aerospace industry, and is a major exporter, decides that it wants to transfer exchange and credit risks as much as possible. It will have to pay to do so, but prefers to bear that cost rather than be exposed to currency swings on large contracts.

Your attitude towards risk might change. For instance, when you're growing market share strongly, you may need to take on additional risk. The challenger bank we mentioned has decided to grow strongly by targeting a relatively high-risk area of the lending market. Once it has acquired a reasonable size loan book, it may decide to move its risk profile down a notch, which it could easily do by tightening up its loan criteria.

Having set an overall strategy, you need to map all the risks to which your business is exposed. All these elements need to be quantified so that you can manage the risk, for instance by hedging the currency exposure. Unless you quantify risks, you can't understand how important they are, or how to manage them. A line in a report from a stockbrokers' analyst that says "The company is an exporter and it has a foreign exchange risk" is not useful to an investor, and this wouldn't be useful management information. A risk manager (or an investor who has done their homework) would say: "The company exports to the European Union and has a $550m Euro exposure." Then they would look at whether that exposure is hedged, and what the impact of a 1% change in exchange rates would be on profits.

For instance, a company that exports consumer goods will be exposed to currency risk and credit risk (where it is extending credit to its customers). Mapping that exposure requires an analysis of the following factors:

- firm and expected orders,

- timing (When are orders received? How long do customers take to pay?)

- the currency in which costs are denominated, and the mismatch with the currency in which payments are received.

Suppose you acquire a foreign company which trades only inside its own country. Its costs and sales are perfectly matched. But if you take out a loan in your own currency, you have a mismatch - if the currency rate changes, its profits might not be enough to pay the interest. Borrow in the other currency, and you have avoided that risk - though of course your accounting profits can still be affected by currency swings.

You might also run a gap analysis. Simply, you're looking at what risks your business now runs, and where you would *like* to be in terms of risk. Are there areas where you could get better returns by running a little more risk, for instance by taking on smaller or less credit-worthy customers in order to increase your sales and gain economies of scale? Are there areas where you are exposed, but you don't want to be?

Proper ERM needs proper risk management frameworks to be set up. Again it's useful to think of the way your financial controls work - how you budget, report and monitor sales and costs. You might set risk limits, above which a decision needs to be referred to the board; you need some method of risk reporting (for instance, continually assessing the amount of sales in a given currency).

In banks which trade on their own account, risk monitoring and reporting is particularly important. The Chief Risk Officer can even order a business unit to reduce, or close out, a risk position, for instance if there is a big market move against the bank or if a trader has overstepped risk limits. Risk positions should be valued daily and an alert set at 85% of the limit. Exception reports are essential, flagging up potential problems before hard limits are hit.

Setting up a framework for risk analysis and control

It's worth looking at what regulations for US public companies have to say about risk management. While the Sarbanes-Oxley Act doesn't address risk management as a separate discipline, it requires the CEO and CFO to disclose any weaknesses in the company's controls. If you don't have an adequate risk management framework, that's a weakness in controls.

Most banks have a Chief Risk Officer who will sit on the management committee and report to the board of directors on risk exposure and how it is being managed. Fund managers and traders will have a risk management team in the front office, so that they can assess their positions in terms of risk, but risk at a corporate level will be managed in the middle office, and it is the back office (where trades are settled and payments handled) that is responsible for reporting. Relying purely on front office risk management is not a great idea, as traders may put pressure on their risk managers to okay a deal - and the front office staff won't have a view of the entire bank's risk profile.

Of course, as with any discipline within an organization, politics starts entering into the equation very quickly. In bond trading, risk and return is transparent, because the ratings and the yield on a bond are known factors. In most areas of risk management, risk is less obvious and there's more room for debate. That gives people a lot of room to fudge. You may see them deny that a particular trade or decision has any risk involved in it, or minimize the risk - or you may see them refuse to allow a particular action because "it's risky", playing up the potential for things to go wrong. Putting your hands in the air, sucking your teeth in saying "oooooooh, risky!" is not a valid risk management technique - it's actually one reason we *need* risk management. We should, equally, point out that risk managers are not there to discourage innovation. They're simply there to point out and manage the risks. Imagine a good risk manager talking to the Wright brothers before their first flights. She wouldn't tell them not to take off - she'd be asking how high the plane would fly, how fast, what safety equipment they could use, whether a first aider would be on hand. A good risk manager will *enable* the business to take risks in a controlled way.

So for instance, a tech firm that wants to move from selling software licenses to Software as a Service runs the risk that it will lose a lot of license income over the next couple of years, as SaaS cannibalizes its sales and support base. On the other hand, of course, it runs the risk that another company will move to SaaS and start to muscle in on its market share. A good risk analysis will ask questions such as: How many license sales do we have to lose before the company falls into loss? Is there a way to phase the transition or to encourage existing customers to move in a controlled manner on to the new platform? The risk manager will at the same time need to look at issues such as how to ensure continuity of service, which might involve inspecting the risk management and business continuity plans of a third party data center.

Watch out for politics, and watch out for incentive schemes which, because they don't have a risk budget, reward high-risk behaviors. If a bank rewards branch managers simply on how many mortgages they can write, without considering credit quality, loan-to-value or other risk factors, managers will be incentivized to take on very poor quality business. A bank that wants to expand its loan book needs to consider the impact on loan quality.

ERM doesn't just concentrate on finding what the risks are. It's about managing them proactively, and the board should get detailed reports on this. For instance, if you're hedging currency risks, then there should be a report on how much the hedge is costing and what effect it has had. (If you are insuring your property, for instance, you need to be certain that you're getting cost-effective insurance; if you are paying out the entire cost of your real estate every five years to insure it, that's not cost-effective.)

However, you shouldn't be monitoring to see whether you're making a profit on your hedge. You should be monitoring to see whether it has worked. In the example of the currency hedges we already mentioned, you would be looking to see whether they protected your profit margin as expected, and whether the match between costs and sales, or between debt payments and the profits of your subsidiary, was as expected, or whether corrective action needs to be taken. Were your initial goals met?

You might have other goals. For instance, a trading desk in a bank might have decided to limit losses to a certain amount per day through actively managing its risks. Has this worked, or is reporting not accurate enough and remedial action not fast enough?

Good ERM will benefit from regular meetings focused on assessing the risk profile of the business. Depending on the size and complexity of your business that might be monthly, or it might be annual, but it's regularity that counts - and having a series of records so that you can go back and ask why you missed a particular risk, or whether your risk management was adequate last year. You also need to report on how robust your risk control environment has turned out to be - just as your finance director might be expected to talk about how the sales force managed to overspend their travel and entertainments budget last year, and how new controls need to be introduced to prevent it happening again.

Evaluating the performance of your risk management strategy closes the feedback loop - and it also helps to convince those managers who're not convinced of the benefits of risk management, if you can point out how the risk strategy actually helped the business.

<u>What risks to control?</u>

Obviously you can't go through life thinking about every single risk you run. Risks that aren't material - like spilling a cup of lukewarm coffee, for instance, or having a shop open a minute late - are not worth worrying about. Part of risk management is about identifying the important risks - you need to prioritize.

Anyone who has looked at financial reports from public companies will be used to reading the boilerplate sections that describe the company's risks. Clearly, they're intended to help investors, but many of them enumerate every risk a business could possibly run -

senior officers might leave the company, it might lose an important client, it could lose its trade credit insurance, interest rates on its debt might go up, there might be a tornado or an earthquake, its products might become obsolete, the sky might fall on Chicken Little's head.

That *doesn't* help investors. In fact sometimes, it's just motherhood and apple pie - investors need to know which of those risks are really major risks right now. For instance, if you are looking at an innovative digital media company with a high profile CEO and CTO, then probably, losing either of those officers would be a much greater risk. Now that's not the kind of risk you can insure against or hedge, but it might make one want to see a good succession plan or experienced independent directors on the board. If on the other hand you're considering an investment in a high street retailer with thin margins, it might be able to afford losing its CEO, but losing its trade credit could be enough for suppliers to stop dealing with the company, and that could push it into bankruptcy. Risk management isn't about enumerating every single risk you can think of - it's about knowing the risks you run and as with every kind of management, concentrating on the most important ones (those which are either very common, or very large).

Who manages the risk?

You may need more than one risk manager. Different types of risk need different skills to manage. An IT company may need someone who can manage operational risk, and is used to dealing with service level agreements, business continuity assessments, and four-nines availability; even within a financial institution, monitoring and controlling the risk of a loan book requires a different skill set from front office management of market risks.

Ensure that the individuals who *incur* risk are held to account for it. But ensure that it is someone else who is responsible for *monitoring* and *controlling* that risk. Otherwise, it's too easy for individuals to game the system or even simply put in false reports.

A note on regulation

Many industries are now highly regulated, not just in finance - pharmaceuticals, foodstuffs, electricals, aerospace and data processing are all tightly controlled by regulations, and regulatory risk is a whole specialist area of risk management. Equally, regulators are becoming increasingly involved in looking at the way the companies they regulate manage risk.

There's a temptation to see regulation as a regrettable nuisance, and either decide to simply tick the boxes ("Yes we've got risk and yes we manage it, it that enough?") or to do what you were going to do anyway and pay any fines that are imposed as a cost of doing business ("Oh dear, we broke that rule, never mind, $250 isn't going to hurt"). But neither of these attitudes is very helpful, and if you do end up with a problem - for instance, a bank that suddenly discovers a very serious problem with a major client account - you're not going to know how to sort it out.

Regulators probably won't become your friends, but if they can see that you are trying to do the right thing and are actively seeking their advice, they are likely to consider your problems more sympathetically. If you have a problem that might end up in front of the regulatory, disclose it before you're forced to, and make sure that you have both the right figures available, and some suggestions as to how you might address the issue and move forward.

Thinking outside the box can actually help you. For instance, if there are blind spots or ambiguities in the regulations, this can represent an opportunity. Think about whether new regulations help or hinder your business; if, for instance, your services already comply with a new regulation that's coming in next year, you can use that fact to win business from competitors.

If you think honestly that regulations are stopping your business from providing a good service, then take it up with the regulators informally. In some cases, regulators - if convinced that what you're doing, though ambiguous in terms of regulation, is right - can actually help you achieve your goals. Don't think of them as the enemy.

One building company noted the increasingly onerous nature of environmental regulation in the construction industry as a risk to their strategy. One way to address that risk might have been to lobby against such measures. Instead, this company decided to tackle green building head-on, marketing their homes on low energy consumption and sustainability, training their contractors to not just become a leading player in the environmental building market, but also to be actively involved in creating the next generation of sustainable building regulations and techniques.

That's done more than simply deliver good PR and more sales. In the refurbishment market, a low-energy refurb is considerably more costly than a 'regular' contract, and delivers better profit margins. So the company has a much higher level of sales on the same number of contracts, and makes more profit as well.

And finally… when you are managing an enterprise's risk, remember that risk is not a 'bad' thing or a 'good' thing, it's something you budget for. It's a bit like selecting which gear you should drive in - first gear isn't better or worse than fifth, but you'd select gear depending on the conditions, where you want to go, how fast, and how much fuel you're prepared to expend to get there. Choose your risk levels strategically, budget for them adequately, and monitor how well you're achieving your objectives - that's ERM in a nutshell.

Chapter 4 – Risk management models and 'The Greeks'

This is another slightly theoretical chapter, as anyone who is managing financial risks needs to have a bit of background in mathematics and economics to understand the basic models that underline modern thinking about risk. Understanding the models is far more important than doing the calculations - there are computer programs that will handle that for you.

<u>Portfolio theory</u>

Now here's a question worth debating: how do investors choose their investments? No doubt some of them just stick a pin in the stocks pages of the Wall Street Journal or the Financial Times, but most of them are looking for an economic reason. Henry Markowitz took a philosophical approach to this question, and his answer is an interesting one. He suggests that investors select their investments to give them the highest return for a given amount of risk.

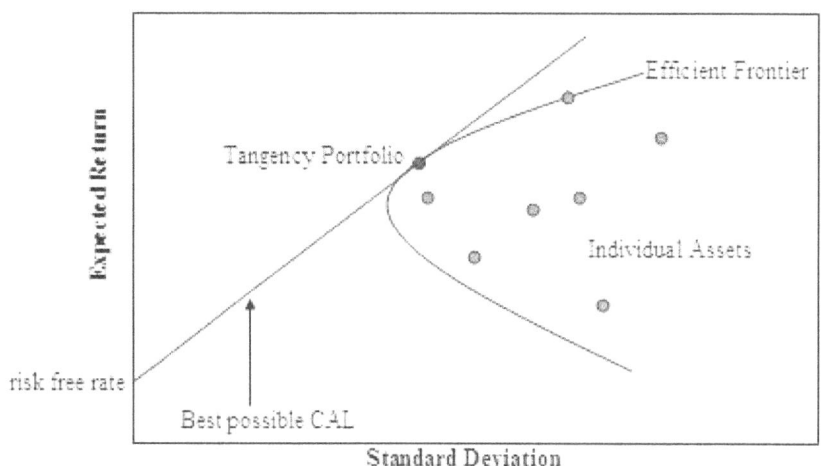

If you plot these investments you get a curve. You're looking at expected return on one axis and the standard deviation of the return (i.e. the risk of that investment) on the other. The curve shows the highest return for any given amount of risk. This is the efficient frontier - no other investments offer a better return for the given amount of risk.

Now what you've got here is thinking about a portfolio rather than about individual investments. It's a way of looking at the way a portfolio can be created and the way that different assets within it interact. In the mid-1960s the idea was developed a bit further into the Capital Asset Pricing Model (CAPM). This looks at the risks involved in an investment portfolio and analyzes them into two kinds: specific risk - the risk of the particular individual investment - and systematic risk, the risk of the entire market as a whole. You can diversify away specific risk - you can't do anything about systematic risk.

Let's take that a bit further. From the efficient frontier, we know that investors weigh their portfolio on a risk/return basis; and we can see that they have a preferred point between the return on the risk-free asset (normally reckoned to be a relatively short dated Treasury - something that has no default risk and little interest rate risk) and the total market portfolio of all risks. They're taking more risk than if they invested in the risk-free asset, and so they demand a premium above the risk-free rate of return as their reward for assuming that risk.

Now let's get stuck into some numbers. The market as a whole - treat it as a portfolio - has a given risk. The price of any asset reflects its contribution to the overall market portfolio risk - its *beta*. The beta of the overall market, of every investment that's available, is 1. A stock may have a lower beta (less volatile - returns on the stock are less variable than market returns - or poorly correlated with the market) or a higher one (a stock that is more volatile and/or highly correlated with the market).

Beta is the *specific risk* that we mentioned earlier - the risk that can't be diversified away. To get technical, it's the covariance between the return on that particular asset and the market, divided by the market variance:

$$\beta = \frac{\text{Cov}(r_a, r_b)}{\text{Var}(r_b)},$$

Another way of seeing it is to look at the expected rate of return on an asset as the risk-free rate, *plus* the investment's beta multiplied by the excess of market return over the risk-free rate. Fortunately, you don't have to do all this calculation yourself; betas on most stocks are available on services like Bloomberg. We'll talk a bit more about how to use them in the chapter on managing risk for assets and portfolios.

alpha, beta, gamma, delta ... theta, rho and vega

We've already looked at beta as a measure of volatility but we should also look at a range of other sensitivities on individual securities. However, though they're useful for thinking about risk on an individual position, they can't simply be added up to come up with a total risk ranking for a portfolio, so they don't help you manage risk overall. They're primarily intended for trading derivatives, such as options - they're highly useful for hedging positions, too, so they have their use in a corporate treasury department that's operating currency or interest rate hedges.

Almost all of these measures are named after letters of the Greek alphabet and so they're often known as 'The Greeks'. Let's start with delta (Δ). This measures the price risk of a derivative compared to the underlying stock. It's a linear exposure to a market factor; so buying the original stock, the delta is 1 - you lose $1 if the price falls $1. With derivatives, delta will vary between -1 and 1 - negative for put options and positive for call options. It's useful not just in derivatives trading, but also in hedging (in fact some people call it the hedge ratio).

Suppose you have a stock selling at $10 and call options on that stock with a delta of 0.4. You pay $3 for the option. If the stock goes up to $20, the option will increase by $10 x 0.4 = $4.

Gamma (γ) is convexity risk. Let's explain that: gamma shows the degree to which delta correlates to the price of the underlying stock. Still confused? Let's explain further: gamma reflects the risk that the delta will change. For instance, when an option moves deeper in-the-money, its delta will increase towards 1, while when it's moving in the opposite direction, out-of-the-money, it will move in the other direction.

Gamma is largest if the option is expiring soon and there's not much time for the price of the underlying security to move, and it's also largest for options that are at-the-money (the exercise price is the same as the stock price). That makes short-term options higher risk than those with longer periods to run.

You might like gamma. Momentum investors, who follow trends, focus on positive gamma opportunities where a big move up will make them money, and use a tight stop loss to get out of losing trades. They love big moves in the market and high volatility; the risk is that the move will go the wrong way.

Other investors hate gamma. Negative gamma investors like markets that are moving sideways, but the risk is that a large move could occur in either direction, up or down. One way of protecting themselves against undue risks of a big move is to trade the spread rather than selling an option - that is, limit the risk by selling an option but buying a less expensive option of the same time.

Vega is volatility risk. It measures the sensitivity of the option value to the volatility of the underlying security. If the stock becomes more volatile, what happens to the option price? Vega expresses the change in the options price for every 1% change in volatility.

(Had you spotted that this measure is the exception to the rule? There is no vega in the Greek alphabet.) Vega is, in a way, a measure of sensitivity to market *expectations*.

Moving on, theta (θ) is a very important factor in options - it represents time decay risk. Is your option running out of time? If you buy a deep out-of-the-money option with two months to run, you may think events will get the price of the underlying security where you need it to be by the time the option expires - if the option has twenty-four hours to run, you're much more unlikely to be saved by a major price move. The option therefore diminishes in value as it approaches expiration, if all else remains equal. Theta aims to quantify this risk.

Of course, if you *write* an option, time decay works in your favor!

Rho, the next of the Greeks, measures the sensitivity of a derivative to a change in interest rates (technically, the risk-free rate of return).

Value at Risk (VaR) model

Value at Risk is a way of considering the total risk of a portfolio. It defines the worst level of expected loss at a given confidence level, assuming that losses and profits are normally distributed. So for instance, daily VaR of $10m at 99% confidence (that's a Basel 2 requirement, by the way) means that your trading book should realize a daily loss above $100m on only one day in every 100.

However, it doesn't quantify by how much the limit will be exceeded. On the one losing day, you might lose $101m, or you might lose $1bn. VaR only tells you about the frequency of a particular loss, not the amount.

VaR is useful in normal markets for managing risk within a single trading day or even up to a couple of weeks, but it's not a great way to measure long-term risks, and it's not very robust when coping with extreme conditions. In fact, some financial experts believe the use of VaR can force banks to liquidate their positions when the market falls, making a bad situation much worse. In a normal market, though, VaR works well as a method of quantifying risk.

To calculate VaR, first calculate the distribution of the portfolio - use historical data to show returns ranked from worst to best, with the extent of loss or gain on the horizontal axis and the number of days such returns were achieved on the vertical axis. You can then choose your confidence level. For instance, for 95% confidence you'd exclude the worst and best 2.5% - the extreme ends of the distribution curve. For 99% confidence, you exclude the worst 0.5% and the best 0.5% of returns. You can then see the level of worst expected loss by reading off the required percentile.

VaR measures risk across all risk factors, at business level and at the level of the firm as a whole. It shows the short term risk appetite of the firm. It's useful as it's a consistent, integrated measure which gives aggregate numbers, and you can measure risk-adjusted performance using it (as you'd calculate return on investment, but here you're looking at return for a given VaR). You can also drill down from the overall VaR numbers to see which business unit is taking most risk.

Where VaR doesn't always help you is in looking at individual areas of risk. Breaking down risk can sometimes be important; for instance, if you have a currency hedge you may need to break it down into interest rate risk, exchange rate risk, and volatility risk. VaR only gives you the top line - you'll need to look at the breakdown separately. And to get the most use out of VaR, it goes without saying that you're going to need a robust control environment and good (and speedy) reporting.

Analytic variance/covariance

Another way of calculating VaR is to assume that returns are normally distributed, rather than looking at historical returns. But you need to look at both the stock price of each stock in the portfolio, and its volatility, *and* the correlation between the two stocks (the correlation coefficient of the pair). With three stocks, you'd have to look at the correlations AB, BC, and AC; with four, AB, BC, CD, AC, AD, BD; with five, all of those plus AE, BE, CE, DE - nine correlations in all. It doesn't take long till the number of correlations you'd need to model gets out of the control.

Another weakness is the assumption of normal distribution. Returns are often 'fat-tailed', that is, skewed, rather than normally distributed.

Historical simulation

Historical simulation can be used for VaR, but it needs at least 2-3 years of data and of course it makes the assumption that the future will look like the past. If there have been structural changes in the market that might not be the case.

Monte Carlo simulation

That's why nowadays most banks prefer to use a Monte Carlo simulation. It's highly computer intensive, but that's not such a problem as it might have been twenty or thirty years ago. The first step is to specify all risk factors. Having done this, price paths for securities are constructed using random number generation. Then the portfolio for each path is valued, at which point the distribution of returns for the entire portfolio can be seen.

While short-term VaR can be reached using any of the calculations we've described, long-term VaR is only possible if you use Monte Carlo simulations.

Chapter 5 – Credit risk management

All banks, by nature, lend money - and so they have credit risk that they need to manage. In retail banking, the products are likely to be mortgages, credit cards, overdrafts, and perhaps also small business loans (often secured on the personal assets of the business proprietor); in corporate banking, they will be loans, both fixed and floating, and might also include asset finance or factoring.

Companies which extend credit to their customers also have a credit risk. If that's a fairly simple risk - a small business making products to sell through multiple retailers - it may not require particularly sophisticated risk management. However, if you think about a contractor who relies on stage payments from customers in five or six different countries, with different amounts of money upfront, you could end up with some quite complex issues of timing and currency risk - and you'd want to manage that a lot more proactively and using rather more sophisticated tools.

Lumpiness - the princess and the pea of credit risk!

Most companies which lend to consumers have loan books consisting of a large number of small, low-value loans. Retail customers aren't linked to each other - if one guy loses his job or borrows too much, the impact will be limited to his own mortgage of personal loan - and default risk estimates are generally pretty reliable.

Corporate loan books, on the other hand, are often 'lumpy', with a smaller number of high-value loans. Actual losses can often vary significantly from default estimates, because of that lumpiness. Corporate loans may also be linked, for instance if the bank lends to both house builders and building materials providers - problems in the construction industry could see both types of borrower defaulting. A single major retailer going bankrupt could take several wholesalers and suppliers with it. If the bank has a high exposure to loans in a particular sector, it's likely that if one customer in that sector has problems, others will, too.

While risk management for both loan portfolios will be similar, a corporate loan book with chunky positions needs much more in-depth analysis - and tighter risk rules.

Only experienced candidates need apply

Experience is a major part of credit risk management - for instance, experience of the loan book and how customers tend to behave. Operationally, a bank will have a good feel for the typical warning signs of default or distress - for instance, a customer fails to make the minimum payment on time, or with credit cards, or a customer who has always paid the full amount monthly changes to paying only the minimum. With trade customers, a supplier knows that if days sales outstanding (DSOs) start to drift out, there could be financial problems at the customer firm, and it's time to think about tightening up credit.

There are a number of ways that problems in the loan book can be addressed:

- Repricing - A bank which is seeing arrears on its mortgage book growing might consider making its mortgages more expensive, or charging a higher arrangement fee, and hoping a higher interest rate deters poor quality customers. This won't affect existing loans, but it will steer the portfolio as a whole in a different direction.

- Changing the risk rules - The bank might also decide to reduce the multiple of salary or the loan to value ratios on which it's prepared to offer mortgages. In the former case, its customers will be paying less of their salary out on the mortgage and so potentially more likely to be able to keep paying - in the latter case, the bank will retain a higher percentage of collateral.

- An exporter which has seen DSOs drifting out might decide to offer a discount for cash (or prompt) settlement.

- It might also decide to reduce exposures, perhaps deciding not to trade with a country where payment delays are excessive, or to limit the trade credit it offers to a particular percentage of its total receivables.

- Marketing strategies could also be changed to target customers more likely to pay on time.

Of course the fact that credit portfolios are managed on the basis of experience raises difficulties when you're dealing with new, innovative products that don't have a track record, or sharp changes in the economy or in a sector. For instance, many lenders have been surprised by the severe impact of e-commerce on major retail chains. A number of major chains, such as Toys R Us, have filed for bankruptcy, and several others have lost their trade credit insurance coverage, meaning suppliers are taking a larger risk selling to them. Tighter risk controls and monitoring are needed when dealing with an industry in crisis, or a new venture.

Another issue with credit portfolios can be a form of *model failure*. In consumer credit and small company loans many of the processes are semi-automatic ("computer says no"), based on credit scores either from third parties or created by the bank itself on the basis of information given by the applicant. It's important to test these models - trace back defaults and arrears to the original credit decision and then see whether there are faults in the system or whether there is a single factor common to all bad loans. Processes need to be thoroughly tested.

Credit scoring

Credit scoring models allow credit processes to be automated, at least partly. They also help the credit process to deliver consistent results, by using statistical techniques to replace (or support) personal judgments. Some banks prefer to use scores from a credit bureau such as FICO, while others aim to gain competitive edge by creating custom models in-house. (As noted above, any such model can represent a risk if it fails to operate as expected.)

Cut-off scores are used to grant or refuse credit, but can also be used for risk-based pricing - that is, offering lower interest rates to higher quality customers. Until recently most credit scores were based on historical data, but there has been a move to real-time and many banks now use dynamic 'behavior scoring' - it's also used by some proptech companies to evaluate tenants. For instance, every month a tenant pays on time, her score goes up.

Models are also becoming more sophisticated. Instead of simply looking at the probability of default, different scorecards are used which can forecast, for instance, how likely a certain type of mortgage customer is to switch out of the mortgage in the short term, attrition rates for credit cards, likely response rates to direct marketing of other products, or total usage of cards. Rather than simply predicting default, it's also possible to predict the profitability of a particular customer in terms of other products they can be sold. The same is true of commercial credit risk - models have evolved greatly in the past ten years or so.

However, the more complex models become, the more important it becomes to test the model and to tie the results back to the original predictions, closing the feedback loop. In particular, you'll want to consider the risk-adjusted return - what return are you making for taking the risk of a loan? Does it adequately compensate the risk? Was the outcome in line with the risk assessment that you had made? The answers to these questions can then be fed back into the bank's ongoing strategy.

Valuation risks

A loan book can include *valuation risk,* if collateral has been secured. For instance, a mortgage lender runs a valuation risk on the properties against which finance has been secured. Usually, the loan-to-value percentage protects the lender, but in booming property markets, loans are sometimes granted at 100% of the value of the property. If the property market crashes, the lender is exposed to the risk of a customer defaulting on the loan *and* the property being worth less than the amount of the loan.

Worse, in markets that are turning downwards, lenders trying to sell collateral further depresses property prices, creating a vicious spiral and leading to an excess inventory of assets for sale that can take years to clear. For instance, after the 2007 credit crunch, the Spanish property market crashed; many banks ended up with huge amounts of property on their books after construction companies and real estate developers went bust. By 2015, there were still 390,000 empty properties awaiting sale, of which the banks held 85%.

Mortgages are not the only loans to suffer valuation risk. Automotive loans and leases have a high valuation risk if a particular model proves not to hold its value well.

There is a high *correlation risk* with such loans. Inevitably, you'll see property companies having problems servicing their loans at exactly the same time that real estate prices are going down. In other words, the value of the collateral correlates with the creditworthiness of the customer; both will typically fall together. Not great news for the bank, and a reason why you need to consider both those risks together.

Bond markets

Credit risk also affects bond markets, though they respond to other drivers besides credit risk. We can consider the major risks:

1. risk of default,

2. recovery rate,

3. credit migration.

Losses are not always, and indeed quite infrequently, 100% - usually a default will lead to a reorganization of debt, or, in the case of an insolvent company, bondholders recovering part of their investment through the liquidation of assets. That's why you need to think about recovery rates as well as the default risk, so the total risk you run is the risk of default times the amount of the loan that is *not* likely to be recovered.

Credit migration is a different risk. While a company might not default, a ratings agency might decide that its creditworthiness is not as good as it was thought to be. When a major agency like Standard & Poors downgrades a bond, the market usually reacts by increasing the yield on the bond - or, if you like, cutting its price. So even a company with a tiny chance of defaulting could pose a major risk of capital loss if its credit rating is cut significantly. It's worth noting that nearly 10% of triple-A rated bonds are downgraded every year, so this is a risk event that's reasonably likely to occur.

A transition matrix is a good way to assess migration risk. The ratings agencies put them out, showing the probability of any given rating migrating to another specific rating by year end. For instance, according to S&P a bond that's AAA rated has a 5.83% chance of being downgraded to AA, but zero chance of being downgraded to B or lower. Using the matrix, you can assess the migration risk involved in your portfolio.

Approaches to measuring the credit risk of a portfolio

There is no holy grail to measuring credit risk. You'll want to look at concentration risk, whether by geography or by sector. You'll want to take a look, too, at the way default rates vary by the economic cycle, and perhaps also by the product life cycle (companies in early stage or in very mature industries with thin margins can have higher default risks than mid-stage businesses).

The maturity of loans also needs to be considered. A shorter maturity loan is generally a lower risk; a loan that will be paid back in six months is much lower risk than one which will only be repaid in ten years. Experience, as so often in this area, is the best way of quantifying that risk.

Hedging and syndication

While a bank may be able to originate loans in different currencies and at both floating and fixed rates, it may not want to take on exchange rate and interest rate risk as well as credit risk. The use of hedging and syndication strategies enables a firm to set its own risk appetite.

Many banks use *Credit Default Swaps* (CDS) to hedge their credit risks. The buyer of the hedge sells the credit risk on to a third party, paying a small amount regularly as 'insurance'; they receive a payout in the event of default. Effectively, that means they are making a return (reduced by the amount of the protection payments) on their money, but they are no longer at risk of default. Obviously, the level of return after payments for the CDS needs to remain above the risk-free rate, otherwise the bank would be better off not making the loan at all. CDSs also offer a bank flexibility in terms of leverage - it can offer additional loans, and increase its market share, without needing to increase its capital. It divorces the risk decision from the credit management decision. Freeing up capital is one of the main advantages of using CDSs.

However, CDS contracts need to be carefully drafted (CDSs are not traded - they're tailor-made contracts). What events trigger a payout?

Is a single missed payment enough, or does the company have to enter liquidation before the payout is triggered?

First-to-default CDSs are also available on a pool of loans - as the name says, they cover the first company of a selected portfolio of loans to default. Under normal market conditions this can be a more efficient way of 'insuring' a selection of loans than securing a CDS for each of them singly.

Another problem with CDSs and similar derivatives is that you have counterparty risk. If you buy your hedge from a bank that is unable to honor it, perhaps because it's written a large number of CDSs that are all being triggered at the same time (e.g. in a major market downturn), you've wasted your money. The number of financial institutions that offer derivatives of this type is quite small, so even if you diversify your CDS holdings, you may still find the counterparty risk comes back to bite you.

Loan syndication is another way of managing the risk of a credit portfolio. A large number of individual loans are packaged together and sold to third-party investors, who benefit from the continuing income stream. CLOs (collateralized loan obligations) and MBSs (Mortgage Backed Securities) enable individual investors to access the income streams from credit portfolios directly and let the bank shift the risk. The price of the package is paid to the originator - effectively canceling out the credit risk by delivering capital repayment ahead of time. That enables the bank to focus on origination (marketing its loans and selecting the best applicants) rather than on risk management for the credit portfolio.

There's a further advantage to CLOs: different tranches can be offered with different qualities of credit. So for instance a pool could offer an A3 tranche, a Baa3 tranche, and an equity tranches - it's the equity risk that makes this "not a free lunch" for investors, of course.

There's nothing wrong with securitization. It started early in the US mortgage market and by the 1990s, 50% of US mortgages were securitized. However, in the sub-prime mortgage boom, many packages had far below the credit quality advertised, while some incautious buyers bought the lowest quality tranches for the high returns available without considering the risk, and got badly bitten when the market turned.

Using ETFs and credit indices

A third way of managing risk on a credit portfolio is to use ETFs and derivatives based on credit indices such as the iTraxx or CDX. Out of these, the iTraxx Europe index is the most frequently traded, mainly in the Over The Counter (OTC) market, though ICE also offers clearing of iTraxx products. This can be a much easier way to manage risk than arranging a CDS for each loan in a portfolio, and is similar to using a currency or interest rate hedge via options or futures.

Chapter 6 – Some aspects of market risk management

Managing market risk is essential if you have any kind of investment assets that are tradable - equities, currency, bonds or commodities. Markets move, and a big move against your position can really damage your wealth, or your business. It's a risk that needs therefore to be analyzed, and then controlled.

As we saw with the CAPM, market risk comes in two types - there's general market risk, and there's instrument-specific risk. The latter can be diversified away by investing in assets with different risk exposures, but general market risk can't be diversified away and has to be accepted, or hedged.

Types of market risk

The type of risk most individual investors are aware of is equity risk - the portion of risk on an individual share that can't be diversified away. If the Dow Jones falls a certain amount, most equities will correlate to that fall in greater or lesser degree. Fortunately, that risk can be hedged, for instance by taking out a put option or buying a short ETF on the relevant market index.

Currency exchange risk is another form of market risk. Because banks are massive traders in currencies, there are a huge number of forms of hedge available, including futures, options, holding an uncorrelated currency, or using currency-hedged ETFs.

Commodity price risk reflects changes in commodities markets, which can be highly specialized. For instance, as well as physical commodities such as wheat, gold, steel, oil or cotton, futures are available on transport movements (e.g. Baltic Dry Freight Index, futures on individual freight routes). While hedges on commodity prices through futures or ETFs will help companies that are exposed to these prices, they may also be of interest to individual investors who have large positions in commodity and energy stocks.

Interest rate risk

Bonds and other debt securities, and to a lesser extent equities (particularly REITs and stocks with high yields) are exposed to a change in interest rates. If interest rates rise, the prices of interest-bearing assets will fall, and vice versa. This risk isn't simple, as it breaks down into two types of risk - *basis risk*, that is, exposure to a simple shift in interest rates, and *curve risk*, exposure to changes in the yield curve.

To analyze these risks we first need to analyze all open positions and look at any mismatches of interest rate or maturity. For instance, you may borrow short term and lend long term, borrow fixed and yield at floating rates, or simply have more money borrowed than lent out. As we saw earlier, interest rate risk can be measured by rho.

Basis risk is easy to understand; if you own $100 of a bond that yields 4%, your coupon is $4. If yields rise to 5%, the bond will reprice so that the $4 coupon represents a 5% yield on the new price. 4 / 0.05 = $80, so you will lose 20% of your capital for a 1% rise in interest rates.

Curve risk is a little more complicated. If you look at interest rates, they vary according to the length of the period for which money is lent out. Normally, bonds which are repayable in the short term have lower rates than longer-term loans. Plot the maturity of the loan against rates on a chart and you will usually get an upward sloping yield curve.

Interest rates can change in parallel, that is, all maturities see a change of the same magnitude. But the curve can also shift. For instance, if economic growth is expected, the yield curve might steepen. If a recession is on the way, the yield curve may become inverted, that is, short-term bonds paying higher yields than longer-term debt. So when you have an interest-bearing asset (or liability) you not only have an interest rate risk, you have curve risk.

You might be hedged against a rise in interest rates of 2% - what is called a *parallel shift* in yields. But that won't hedge you against a change in the shape of the yield curve - whether it steepens, flattens, or inverts.

Liquidity risk

Many of the worst busts in the financial world have come about not through a decline in prices or increase in interest rates, but because a *liquidity risk* has crystallized. For instance, a mismatch in funding is a huge risk.

If a bank lends long term, but is funded by short-term assets, a rise in defaults could be difficult to cover. British bank Northern Rock pursued a highly aggressive strategy in the mortgage market, which it funded by heavy borrowing on the wholesale money markets. Northern Rock's assets were short term, while its mortgages frequently had terms of 20-25 years. In 2007, when the bank was unable to borrow from the money markets, it had a liquidity crisis on its hands. Although the Bank of England bailed it out in the short term, depositors who learned of the crisis started to withdraw their money - often forming long queues for ATM machines or outside bank branches - and in 2008, the bank had to be nationalized in order to prevent its complete collapse.

Chapter 7 – Operational risk management

Think of the great rogue trader scandals - the Barings Bank collapse of 1995, Jerome Kerviel's massive losses at Credit Suisse - and you see why operational risk management is so important. However tightly you manage market risk and credit risk, it only takes one rogue trader to bust your bank wide open.

In a finance business, you need to take operational risk management very seriously. It might include any of the following risks:

- fraud

- IT outages or systems faults

- human error ('fat finger' when a trader types in extra zeros)

- natural disaster

In a trading business, you run many of the same risk but also need to add, for instance;

- health and safety issues ranging from driver accident to full-scale explosion of chemical plant,

- supplier insolvency

- logistics issues.

You'll also want to consider business issues such as legal/regulatory risk, strategic risk, and reputation risk. Many other risk events can bring reputation risk with them - for instance, a chemical leak into a local river could result in a business being vilified as a polluter, unless it demonstrates its responsible approach by getting involved in a thorough clean-up; IT outage at a bank that causes customers to miss their mortgage repayments, or be unable to access their funds, could result in the bank being seen as both poorly managed and as not caring about its customers.

The first step to operational risk management, as with financial risk management, is to map the business processes and develop some basic risk metrics in order to quantify both the probability and the likely size of risks. You'll also need to develop a robust reporting framework so that managers who experience problems can't sweep them under the carpet. Then you can think about how to manage those risks.

Why did Barings fail?

Trader Nick Leeson had risen through the Barings trading room to become head of trading in Singapore. But by 1995 his golden touch had deserted him. With the right risk management framework, Barings' management would have seen that he was doing badly, and trimmed the positions he was allowed to take.

However, failings in the risk management process meant that Leeson was responsible for checking his own trades - no one supervised them. He had been able to hide his bad trades in a secret account. It was only when the Kobe earthquake and consequent Asian market collapse drove a stake through the middle of his overnight straddle (a bet that the market wouldn't move much one way or the other) that he was driven to desperately trying to trade his way out of trouble - and failed. His failure was followed by that of the bank he worked for, which had lost over twice its total capital on his trades.

Look for key risk drivers. For instance, when you're considering the probability and severity of an IT outage you might look at the average age of your computer systems, any dependencies of one system on another, total internet traffic in Tb, average percentage downtime for the system, and so on. Look for bottlenecks that can exacerbate risk - could the failure to source one small component bring your entire production system to a standstill?

Now let's think about how to manage risk. Unlike credit or market risk, operational risk is a pure value destroyer. There is no business reason for taking on higher operational risk - it's always bad - one of the few risks that is!

Elon Musk's approach

Elon Musk has a rather different attitude to operational risk, but it's interesting to see how he manages it. While NASA wants to be 100% sure about every component before launching a rocket, Musk's company SpaceX doesn't mind losing a rocket or two - in fact the company has published a video of its worst failures, and it makes great viewing with plenty of explosions and crashes.

But Musk reckons it's better to make lots of (relatively) cheap rockets and lose a few, and learn by the mistakes, rather than to keep making plans and prototypes without real-world testing. Note, though, unlike NASA, he's not putting human beings on board his rockets. So if they crash and burn, no one (except perhaps his bank) gets hurt.

Some operational risk can be mitigated. That can come in the form of controls (for instance, a computer system could be programmed to recognize mismatches of trades, so that when a trader enters a buy order for 100,000 shares and a put option on 1m shares, it flashes up a confirmation screen, thus potentially avoiding a 'fat finger' incident). It might involve safety equipment, access controls (stopping unqualified staff from entering a highly controlled laboratory environment, for example), or quarantining particular processes.

Other operational risk can be transferred, in a number of ways. The most obvious and the most commonly used is insurance, which is basically a form of risk sharing between different policyholders. Insurance has evolved a long way beyond the simple sharing of risk by creating a fire insurance pool, but the principle remains the same.

However, the cost of insurance always needs to be considered. Some companies find that it is more efficient to self-insure for particular risks, or up to a certain amount. In a personal context, a reasonably wealthy person might opt to save money on travel insurance by accepting a higher level of excess - that is, deciding they'll cover their own costs if their luggage gets lost, and insuring only against serious medical emergency.

A business can also transfer risk by creating a joint venture with another company. Suppose I want to produce self-driving cars but I'm worried about a major class action by people who have accidents involving these vehicles. That could break my business. On the other hand, if I set up a joint venture with another producer, it's only the joint venture's funds that are at risk.

Outsourcing or offshoring some operations can also help transfer risk. Many companies have transferred dangerous or polluting processes offshore to countries where fines are lower or even totally absent, and the cost of an accident would be lower. Royalty structures can also be used to make a profit from intellectual capital while transferring the risk of production and inventory holding.

Chapter 8 – Hedging your bets

You may decide that for some of the risks you run, you want to construct a hedging strategy. Remember, hedging is about risks that you don't want to take on, but it enables you to keep the risks that you don't mind running - for instance, an equity fund manager may say "Hey, I'm meant to be good at picking stocks, not trading currencies". So she won't try to hedge the equity risks in the portfolio, but she'll look for some kind of hedge against the currency risks.

You're basically dismantling the risk structure. If you want to invest in Chinese tech companies because they represent a fast growing market, but you're worried about Renminbi devaluation, you can take out a hedge. Or if a European fund manager wanted to hold the FANGs (Facebook, Amazon, Netflix and Google) without running dollar risk, he could simply sell dollars short enough to hedge that aspect of the portfolio. Then you're investing in tech - not in dollars.

You might want to take on credit risk because you think junk bonds are cheap, trading at a larger spread against treasuries than the historical average. But if you buy non-investment-grade bonds, you run an interest rate risk too. You can hedge that out by shorting treasuries, for instance, so that if interest rates rise, your short position will make money to offset the negative impact on your junk bonds. You have successfully disentangled the entwined risks and now you only have credit risk, not interest rate risk.

You also need to remember that hedging, like any insurance, costs money. Not only will you pay for the hedge, but it will take out the possibility of a windfall profit from the exposure. If interest rates fall, and you've hedged your interest rate risk, you won't make money on your junk bonds from the resulting revaluation - you'll only make money if you were right about credit spreads tightening. So you always need to check, not just that the hedge is achieving what you meant it to, but that it's delivering it in a cost-efficient way.

Keeping a hedge current requires cash, because you'll need to buy new options when old ones expire. You'll also need to monitor the hedge so that it keeps up with events. For instance, if you sell some of your assets, you'll want to trim the hedge.

A company hedging its raw materials costs might do so by buying forward. The hedge would naturally cover a certain proportion of expected costs, and it's good practice to layer a hedge over time. For instance, 100% of known requirements would be covered (e.g. where a sales contract has already been agreed or the cost inputs have been contracted for), but perhaps only 25-30% of next year's potential costs. Obviously you'll need to update that hedge on a rolling basis.

A rolling hedge works well in a normal market 'in backwardation' (when the spot price is higher than the futures price) as it makes a profit on rollover. However, if the market is 'in contango' when future deliveries are higher priced than delivery today, you'll make a loss on rollover. That means there's a curve risk as well as the basis risk when you have a rolling hedge. Your choice if the curve does move against you is:

1. liquidate the hedge - this will cost money and use cash, which may be difficult if your assets are falling in price

2. refinance and continue the hedge - this may depend on the support of your lenders

3. sell the hedge to another firm (but then you're no longer hedged, of course), or

4. unwind the original contracts so that the hedge is no longer required.

If a hedge isn't monitored regularly, it's quite possible for a mismatch to occur between the assets and the hedge. You could end up with a hedge position much larger than the assets being hedged, in which case you have an unhedged risk exposure you didn't expect. Hedges going wrong can result in bankruptcy, so hedging is not a magic bullet - it won't save you from poor risk management, and in fact, if your risk management is bad, it could be your hedge that puts the final nail in your coffin.

Chapter 9 – Managing assets and portfolios

Investments

Remember the efficient frontier proposed by Markowitz? One of the big take-outs for investors is that you need to think about every investment in terms of how it relates to your other investments. From a risk management point of view it's not enough to be a stock-picker; you need to have a helicopter view of your portfolio and understand how stocks correlate to each other, how much you have diversified specific risks, and non-equity risks that could impact your investments (e.g. currency risk or interest rate risk). That's something most books aimed at personal investors don't cover, preferring to focus on fundamental investment or momentum trading / technical analysis, both of which concentrate mainly on individual positions.

Diversification is the first lesson to learn, and though most people know it as "don't put all your eggs in one basket," there's significantly more to it than that. Technically, you need to quantify the correlation coefficient of each pair of assets in the portfolio (-1 being a perfect negative correlation, two assets whose prices will move in exactly opposite directions, and +1 being a perfect positive correlations, two assets whose prices will move in lock-step). By ensuring that investments are not all positively correlated with each other, you can reduce the overall volatility of the portfolio, protecting it against a decline in any one asset class, geography or sector.

Diversification can, of course, be carried out on a 'suck it and see' basis, as many private investors do. But at the very least, you should be aware of the currency, geographical and sector balance in your portfolio, and compare that to the market benchmark so that you fully understand any bias in your portfolio. It may well be that you decide to take that bias on, because you have a particular view; one thirty-year-old software consultant has a far higher percentage of her portfolio in emerging market shares than the benchmark, but says, "I'm young, I earn a lot of money, I can take a higher risk, and I'm investing for the long term - so I'm going where the growth is." (It's fair to point out that as a regular monthly investor she also benefits from averaging down - if the markets fall in the short term, she simply buys more units in her chosen funds as a result.) If, on the other hand, like one neurosurgeon, you were to find out you had four times more healthcare stocks in your portfolio than the benchmark, simply because you came across those investing ideas in your job, it would be time to restructure your investments.

Continuous monitoring is the heart of good risk management and that's true of personal portfolios. Remember, you're looking at the structure of asset allocation, not at individual stocks. "Oh look, my NetEase shares have done really well!" is not a risk management friendly comment. "Oh, gosh, my NetEase shares now represent 35% of my net worth, that's a lot for an individual stock; that's a risk for my portfolio, so I might think about reducing it," is more what we're looking for here.

You have several ways to reduce that risk.

- If you have spare cash, investing in other stocks. And not just other stocks, preferably, but stocks that aren't in the tech sector and perhaps correlate negatively to the tech sector.

- If you don't, reducing the NetEase position to a percentage that you're more comfortable with. This is not about "selling your winners," remember - the salient point isn't that the shares have gone up, but that they represent a higher proportion of your total investment than you're comfortable with. You now need to decide what percentage you want to keep, and sell down to that level. If you're aggressive, you might keep the stock as a 20% block - if you're less aggressive as an investor, you might think it was safer to reduce to 10% of the total portfolio.

- Buying a put option against your NetEase shares to protect yourself against a given amount of downside. You could buy a put that's out-of-the-money and pays off if the shares fall more than 10% - that protects you from a major downwards re-rating if, for instance, the company misses an earnings forecast. Be careful, though, to work out what the option is costing you - if it's too expensive you may forgo your gains in paying for the protection.

We should stress that the risk management decision is completely separate from the investment decision. Now, it may so be that when you look at your portfolio you're doing both jobs. And perhaps when you look at NetEase you see that there's an increase in debt and a decrease in margins that haven't been picked up by the analysts but that worry you - so you decide *as a fund manager* that you're going to lighten that holding. But that's a different decision from the *risk manager's* reduction in the position to a lower level. Try to remember which hat you're wearing at any given time - even if it's by a tactic as basic as drawing a line down the middle of a page and putting your FM comments on one side and your RM comments on the other.

Remember that diversification isn't just about having stocks in different sectors. It's about having stocks that react differently to different drivers. For instance, suppose you picked five house builders and five infrastructure stocks... looking at that portfolio from a risk management perspective would show you that you've got a really heavy exposure to interest rates. (With many infrastructure companies, prices are linked to inflation, and values are worked out on a discounted cash flow basis which often builds the prevailing interest rate into the discount rate.) So, a risk manager would ask whether you're prepared to make the call on interest rates, or whether you'd prefer to be hedged against an increase in rates that could damage your investments.

You'll also want to think about *alpha* and *beta*. Beta, as we saw earlier, measures the systematic market risk that attaches to each of your investments - the risk inherent in them because they are traded assets. Beta is the return part of the risk/return formula - it's the return for risk assumed by an investor, which could be you, or anyone else in the market. Alpha, on the other hand, is return you earn for yourself alone, in competition with other investors - it's stock-picking return, it's the *extra* return by which you outperform the market. That's why one of the best sources of investment wisdom is called *Seeking Alpha.*

Another way of looking at alpha and beta: your risk on beta is a sudden, extreme move in the market; your risk on alpha is that you got your stock pick wrong.

Your investment return is the sum of the risk free rate + beta + alpha (RFR + β + α if you like prefer). If you're only making the risk free rate plus beta, you're not as good a fund manager as you thought. If you're only making the risk free rate, it may be time to hand your funds over to a professional (unless, of course, it's a single year's atypically bad performance, which can and does happen to everyone).

Smart beta styles of investing have become more popular over the past decade. A smart beta style creates an alternative market index to capture market inefficiencies. For instance, once might create an index weighted by revenues or profits rather than market capitalization - this should avoid investing in stocks which are overvalued by the market. A risk-weighted index can be created by adjusting the index to take account of individual investments' volatility. Smart beta has been particularly popular in the ETF market - Invesco Powershares reckons 12% of total ETF assets are now represented by smart beta investment.

Finally, let's mention a slightly different way of looking at the risk in your portfolio. This is the *barbell strategy*. Instead of trying to achieve a moderate risk by investing in moderately risky investments, it achieves moderate *portfolio* risk by investing in the two extremes as far as the components of the portfolio are concerned. You put a percentage of your assets into very conservative investments with a low risk - risk free assets or very short dated, high quality bonds - while reserving a small percentage of your portfolio for more aggressive assets.

With a bond portfolio, for instance, part of the portfolio holds very short dated bonds which are not exposed to the risk of capital loss. The other part holds bonds with 10 years maturity or longer, which should deliver a higher return but run a higher risk. Of course, this version is a lot of work, because you'll need to be fairly active in swapping out your maturing short-term bonds for new ones. For an equity portfolio, you might hold lower risk ETFs for 70% of your investments, and focus the remainder of your investments in emerging technologies and emerging markets. That's rather less work - and the work is focused on the area of your portfolio where you'll probably deliver the highest returns.

Asset allocation

Developing our thinking on investment portfolios, remember that asset allocation has a huge place in determining returns. Thinking about asset allocation, you should include your total balance sheet in the mix - all assets and all liabilities. If, for instance, you own outright a large and valuable house, you're probably overweight the residential property market. That could mean you'd want to focus your other investments on areas that are not correlated to interest rates or to the construction and real estate markets, such as technology or consumer goods, or short term bonds.

It's worth noting that asset allocation can see an investment in a number of different ways, and slice a portfolio up in different ways, too. For instance, growth and value stocks will tend to behave differently, so you might allocate portions of your equity investment to each; dividend payers and non-dividend payers will also tend to react differently to market changes. You might look at interest rate sensitive vs interest rate insensitive investments, or high beta vs low beta investments - but in each case, you're thinking about your total wealth, rather as a bank thinks about its total balance sheet.

Asset/liability management

Financial institutions manage their balance sheets in order to minimize risks while optimizing net interest income. Asset Liability Management (ALM) is used on banking book or corporate treasury the way VaR is used on a trading book, to analyze, quantify and manage risk.

The first stage is to find out whether assets and liabilities are matched, or mismatched. For instance, imbalances between assets of shorter and liabilities of longer maturities, between different interest rates, or fixed and floating rates need to be assessed as presenting a risk. Deposits with shorter maturity than loans can present a problem - if interest rates rise, depositors with easy access or 30/60 day accounts need to be paid more, but you can't always increase the rate on longer-term loans.

Gap analysis looks at the difference between rate sensitive assets and rate sensitive liabilities. It can't be carried out just on the overall figures; both assets and liabilities need to be categorized by maturity (the time to repayment, or to repricing, whichever is shortest), and each maturity needs to be matched. For instance, you'll compare assets and liabilities with 1-3 months maturity, at the short end, then

3-6 months, 6-12 months, and so on. Each 'time bucket' needs to be netted off to arrive at the total risk of that bucket.

However, gap analysis won't identify curve risk. It also doesn't take account of forex risk. So you'll need to do separate analysis to find and manage these risks.

You could move on to EaR - earnings at risk. This measures net interest income divided by volatility - it answers the question "for a 1% rise in interest rates, how much do we lose?"

You calculate EaR by multiplying the gap between assets and liabilities by the change in the rate of interest, and then by the repricing gap. So for instance, let's look at a bank that has a single asset, a 10-year T-bond producing 5%, and a single liability base of 6 month CDs yielding 2%. That's a difference of 3%, the bank's margin.

If the rate changes 100 basis points (=1%) then the T-bond won't change. That rate is set. The CDs won't change for six months, but then the rate will increase from 2% to 3%. The bank's margin is now only 2%. So we can calculate the impact on a full year's earnings: (assuming the bond and CDs represent $100k each to give us a nice round number to work with) -

$$100,000 \times [(6/12 \times 0.03) \times (6/12 \times 0.02)] = 100,000 \times (0.015 + 0.01) = \$2,500$$

against the previously expected earnings of $3,000. We can now see that earnings will be down by 16.7% for each 1% rise in interest rates.

With a more complex balance sheet, you'd need to carry out that analysis for each separate time bucket, but essentially the formula is the same - do it for each time bucket and then add the rates together.

Duration

Duration is potentially a better approach as it includes the cash flow characteristics of the portfolio - the size and timing of cash flows. If the portfolio includes assets such as zeros (repayment being the only cash payment), and deposits that pay annually as well as monthly, it's useful to look at the real cash flows rather than the theoretical interest rate differentials. It still doesn't include curve risk, though, so it's not perfect as a risk model.

The formula uses the market value of both assets and liabilities. Duration measures the sensitivity of an asset to a hike in interest rates, expressed as a number of years; it's complex to calculate, but bonds and mutual funds that invest in bonds contain this information in their prospectuses. A duration of one year means that a 1% change in interest rates will see a 1% change in the price of the asset. Two years means a 1% change in interest rates will see a 2% change in the price of the asset, and so on.

Duration is a useful tool for assessing portfolio risk on a bond portfolio. It shows how exposed the whole portfolio is to interest rate risk, so a fund manager can, for instance, trim the duration if she thinks interest rates are headed upwards. Of course, it doesn't have anything to say about credit risk - you'll need to look at that separately.

Caution: hot

Finally, let's consider a bank's assets in terms of 'temperature'. Some funds are, by their nature, very stable long-term funds; for instance equity shares to which shareholders have subscribed. That money isn't going anywhere. Preference shares and term notes are also very stable. On the other hand negotiable CDs and funds secured through the wholesale markets are much less stable. By weighting your assets according to their nature, you're looking at how stable your funds are - and whether you're at risk of a liquidity crunch. You can award funds a score from 1 to 4, for instance:

1. stable money - equity, preference shares, long-term finance

2. DDAs, MMAs and savings

3. wholesale market funds

4. brokers, dealers and negotiable CDs.

Multiply the value of each type of asset by the liquidity risk to quantify how high the risk is you're running. This is a pretty bootstrap kind of measure but it helps focus on the liquidity profile and identify any deterioration in the balance sheet.

Most individual investors probably don't have to worry about liquidity risk much with regard to their stock portfolio. But there are a few areas where you'll need to think about liquidity.

- Some open-ended mutual funds, such as those investing in real estate, may be unable to meet redemptions in a downturn, meaning you won't be able to get your money out. This happened in the 2007 downturn, for instance, and again in 2016 in the UK when the referendum vote to leave the EU led to turmoil in the property markets.

- Trading on margin exposes you to liquidity risk since you can be called on that margin at any time.

- Some types of investment require cash injections, e.g. if you want to continue a rolling hedge. Make sure you budget for such requirements.

Liquidity risk is easily missed out and it's one of the most dangerous risks around for an investor because it can lead to your having to stop out a winning position or sell profitable investments to fund an unprofitable one.

Chapter 10 – Losses and limits

Losses and limits are great ways to control risk, whether you're a major company, a small business, a bank, a trading desk or an individual investor. The key is to decide the losses and risks that are acceptable, and to build an adequate control system that can't be bypassed or subverted. In thinking about limits, you want to set parameters in size, rather than simple yes/no, and you want to encourage *intelligent* risk-taking - that's how you make money, after all.

Maximum drawdown on funds is becoming increasingly popular as a ratio with investors - though it's not the most scientific way of assessing risk. That shows investors are now becoming aware of risk and loss control as important factors in generating the return on investments. This chapter shows you the basic methods of control.

Stop-losses

Setting a stop-loss limits losses to a certain budgeted amount. When you're right you can collect your profits; when you're wrong, you limit the amount you can lose.

What's the right stop point? That partly depends on the nature of your investment. If you're a buy-and-hold investor then maybe you set it at a quite large figure, because the market can go up and down quite a bit, but you're holding the stock on the basis of the long-term fundamentals. One way of thinking about it is at what point does a market fall make it likely that your original view was wrong - how big does a stock price decline have to be for you to think that there's a factor you didn't know about, or that your assessment of the situation was wrong? For instance, you invested in what you thought was a recovery stock. It goes down 5%; you're not worried. Markets are markets. It goes down 10%: you're concerned. It goes down 20%: at this point, you say, I'm pretty sure there's some bad news I haven't heard yet. You'll set a stop-loss at somewhere between 15-20%, perhaps.

On the other hand if you're trading short-term movements you might set a much tighter stop loss. Warning: a tight stop loss can mean that a flash crash will stop you out of a trade that would otherwise have made money, so don't set them *too* tight.

It's worth considering a *trailing stop*. A simple stop loss will stop you out when the asset falls to 20% below the price at which you bought it. A trailing stop will stop you out whenever the price of the asset falls to 20% below peak - so it will keep rising if the price rises, but protect you from the price falling back to your original price or below.

Don't set take-profits levels. Many investors set target prices, for instance expecting a company to be re-rated to the same price-earnings ratio as its competitors, or expecting a credit spread to narrow. But once the target price has been hit, re-rating can continue as more investors become aware of the attractions of the investment - or, indeed, as a company starts to improve its earnings. If an investment hits its target price, that might be a cue to revisit your reasons for investing and see if they still apply - but if they do, it's not time to sell.

You'll want to evaluate your stop-losses from time to time. If you have too high a percentage of stops, you could be losing trades that would become profitable given a bit more leeway. If you don't have enough trades that are stopped out, your stops may be far too loose, so they're not really working for you, and you have capital sitting in failed trades that should really be closed, and the capital put to use in potentially more profitable ways.

Don't confuse a stop-loss control with stop-loss *orders* at a broker. These may be useful if you can't monitor the market constantly; they're basically an order to sell if the price of an investment dips below a certain price. The order is inactive when submitted, and is only actioned if the envisaged circumstances occur.

A variant on stop-loss is the time limit on positions. For instance, you might decide to sell a stock if it doesn't start to move upwards within a month - for instance if you're a momentum investor. Obviously, though, this kind of limit would be anathema to buy-and-hold investors.

Drawdown control

Stop-loss relates to individual investments or trade; drawdown control relates to the whole portfolio, and is intended to reduce the potential portfolio loss. Most major portfolio drawdowns reflect market situations in which the individual investments are correlated, and all suffer at the same time, so drawdown control is intended to cut risk when a portfolio is losing money (based on its peak value). You cut risk when a portfolio loses money from peak, and then you assume more risk when performance begins to improve.

For drawdown to work properly you need to establish *baseline risk*, a target volatility level. Be clear that you are cutting *risk*, not necessarily cutting positions. You might reduce positions and increase cash, or you might reduce just the most volatile stocks. You're not aiming to cut risk to zero, but perhaps by 20-40%. Imagine, if you like, a sailing boat; when the wind blows more strongly you reef the sails, reducing the amount of canvas that's being used, but you don't put down the anchor. Drawdown control is a pretty similar technique - trimming, rather than chopping.

The floor for drawdown control - the amount of loss at which it is activated - should be set *before* the portfolio has problems with liquidity or investor redemptions, but at a level that you don't expect to see in normal market conditions. (Look at the distribution of returns, as you did for VaR, to see roughly what 'normal' looks like.)

Be sensible about how quickly you can respond, particularly if you're a private investor with a day job. How complex is the portfolio? How frequently do you monitor it? Will prices move further against you before you're able to trade? And remember that you'll want to go risk-on again once the markets calm down, so you'll want to have a definition of what you consider to be normal markets - how will you decide at what point to start pushing up the average risk of the portfolio again?

Operational limits

Good risk management depends on limit setting. For instance, a bank might want to think about what level of CDS spread is too much, and what would make it stop doing business with a counterparty. A trading desk might have overall limits, as well as limits on each individual position.

Limits also need to be policed, and there needs to be a defined action to take in the case of breaches of limits. For instance:

- limit - no one stock to account for over 20% of the portfolio

- policing - through weekly reports: alert at 18%, stop at 20%

- action - 18%, discussion of why the stock is such a high proportion of the portfolio; 20%, corrective action - reduction of stake.

While active breaches are most common, e.g. on a trading desk, you also need to watch out for passive breaches - where trades were originally in line with the limits, but where market conditions have changed the original risks for the worse.

Exactly the same framework of risk control will work in a trading company. For instance there might be limits on the amount of credit granted to any single customer. You'll need to think about corrective action, though - simply canceling an order isn't very customer-friendly. It might be better to set an advance control level at which you'd escalate to the board, and ask whether to ignore the limit for this particular customer, to take on the business but secure trade insurance, or to talk to the customer and perhaps limit their ordering ability. (After all, the limit might have simply been breached because of a pipeline effect, if the customer is pre-ordering stocks for the holiday season.)

As always, close the feedback loop by going back to see whether corrective action worked the way it should have done. If you sold down an overweight position in your portfolio; how easy was it to sell? Could you get the market price? Should you have set an alert earlier? Was the adjustment too late or was the limit too large?

<u>Stress testing</u>

Stress testing and scenario analysis are used by banks to ensure their business can withstand extreme market events. They're like a cross between a fire drill and the chair in every Ikea store that's being punched and prodded by mechanical arms to show how robust the chair is. A simpler version of stress testing can help a small company or individual investor think through the major areas of exceptional risk facing them.

Stress testing complements VaR. VaR is about the frequency of losses of a certain size. Stress testing is about size - the bigger the better, so to speak. You're looking at whether your bank can withstand a major market crash or a downturn in the real estate market, let/'s say. You're not going to take a ridiculously implausible case, like a snowstorm closing the Mumbai stock market, but you want an extreme case - such as, for instance, snow stopping planes landing in New York or London for a week. (That's a stress test for one airline catering company.)

Remember that when things go wrong, more than one thing usually goes wrong at once. One failure can lead to others. A stock market crash will give rise to liquidity issues; interest rates could well go up as a result, leading to bond market losses; currency rates might change, too, as a result of the changes in interest rates. A change in interest rates could reduce valuations in real estate (based on yield), and if the real estate market crashes, two or three banks with high exposure in the sector might start to look exposed, so again, the stress could spread.

You're looking at events many times the standard deviation of market changes. The 1987 stock market crash saw prices falling 23% - the normal daily standard deviation is only just over 1%. The failure of LTCM was an 8 SD event, and Goldman Sachs reckoned the 2008 financial crisis saw, according to the CFO, "things that were 25-SD moves, several days in a row." So this is an area of risk where normal distribution curves can't be relied on.

Look at events other than the market - 9/11, Hurricane Sandy, ebola, bird flu, the Kobe earthquake (which indirectly ruined Barings). Build a model of that event's consequences in the market - its impact on currency, interest rates, trade.

Run that stress test - take your current business stats and processes and try to model the impact. Do you survive? If not, why not? Look at the impact on your normal processes; what could you do differently? Could you take action earlier, or take a different action? Then re-run the failed stress test. Once you know what you're doing, you can start building a contingency plan.

A stress test doesn't have to be right one hundred percent. Some banks saw the 2007-8 financial crisis was a lot larger than they'd stress-tested for, but even so, they knew how to hedge, and how and where to cut their positions. Some things didn't work out exactly as expected. But without the stress tests, many more banks would probably have gone under.

Perhaps the best reason of all for stress testing is that in any business, risk management often gets done in 'silos'. There's a guy who knows about operational risk, and another girl in the trading department who understands the risk of derivatives; there's a strategist whose job is about predicting global economic trends and risk and there are risk managers in the back, middle, and front office, and they don't always talk to each other. If you're stress-testing, you have to get them all together, because you're going to be asking questions like "can we actually cope with that level of trades?" or "what if Argentina defaulted again?"

Chapter 11 Instruments for managing risk

We've talked about different instruments for managing risk all the way through this book, but now we're going to collect them in a single chapter so you can easily refer to them. Many are derivatives of one sort or another. Of course, while you can use derivatives for risk management, you can also use them to speculate, and while in 2004 then Fed chairman Alan Greenspan considered derivatives as a source of strength, other commentators are not so sure. Some have even suggested that the 'derivatives tail wagging the market dog' has led to higher volatility.

Some types of instruments are privately contracted, like most credit default swaps and forwards contracts. Where there is no central marketplace, there is a higher default risk and less regulation to protect investors. Other types of instruments are publicly traded. Some markets are professional, others are open to private investors. Each type of instrument has its own methods of valuation and trade, so you'll need to acquire expertise on whichever ones you use. (Fortunately, many marketplaces and providers put large amounts of information at customers' disposal, and for free.)

Major marketplaces for traded instruments are CBOE (equity and other options), Philadelphia (forex options), Chicago Board of Trade (indices and commodities), and Chicago Mercantile Exchange (forex futures). Many stock exchanges also offer options, and ETFs are traded across multiple exchanges.

Forwards lock in a future price. Basically you are buying or selling 'forward', like a farmer selling in October the tomatoes that will be ready next July. A forwards contract is customized, so it's useful for companies that trade in the relevant commodities or currencies. There is an obligation to deliver (or accept) the physical goods on the settlement date, and while no cash is handed over before that date, it must then be settled in full.

Futures are similar to forward contracts in that they obligate the buyer to purchase, or the seller to provide, the relevant asset (or cash) at the close of the contract, at the predetermined price. However, unlike forwards, they are standardized and can be traded on a futures exchange.

Someone opening a futures position will need to provide margin on opening, and further margin can be required if the price moves against their position. Futures are valued by the divergence from original price and the contract is cash settled at maturity on the difference; for instance, if you expect a 3% bond rate you'd buy a contract at 97 (100 - 3 percent), and if at the end of the year the real rate is 4% the future is worth 96 (100 - 4 percent). If you have bought a *long future*, the seller must pay 97-96 = 1.

Options are optional! That is, they're unlike forwards and futures in that you can simply let an option lapse; there is no obligation to exercise it. Traded options are available on standardized terms through many exchanges, and can be used as a hedge on an investment portfolio. For instance, I've got a $250,000 portfolio invested in emerging technology companies - I don't want to sell any of my positions, as in the long term I see these companies growing mighty fast, but I think there's a market correction coming and I want some protection. I can buy a put option on the DJIA, which pays out if the market falls below a certain price, and this is my 'insurance'. (By the way, buying a put rather than selling part of my investments can also save me considerable amounts of capital gains tax.)

You can either buy or *write* options. If you buy a call, you're going long - it will pay out if the price of the underlying goes up to or exceeds the strike price. If you buy a put, you'll make a profit if the price of the underlying falls below the strike price. (When you write an option, the reverse applies. Note that writing a call exposes you to potentially infinite losses, because there's no limit to the amount that an underlying security could rise. We don't recommend it - at least, not without considerable protection. 'Naked' call writing is a dumb game.)

Suppose in my example the market doesn't fall and my option is worthless by the time it expires. I lose my money. However, I need to think of that money not as an investment that failed, but as an insurance payment. It did what it was meant to; it insured my portfolio, and I paid a cost for it.

There are more advanced ways of using options, such as using them to value 'slices' of probability distributions, or making a bet on increased volatility through a straddle (a put and call at the same price). A straddle may seem counter-intuitive, but it can be used to insure against an event you know will happen but about the outcome of which you're deeply uncertain, such as a rate-setting meeting of the Fed, or an election. Caps, floors and collars can also be used, as can average price options (which lower volatility) and knock-in/knock-out, which can be exercised or expire if the price hits a certain level.

Binary options are not a form of hedging, they're a kind of gambling. Leave them alone.

Insurance is a way of transferring operational risk. While most of us are used to home and motor insurance, there are many much more specific insurances available, generally through insurance brokers. For instance, event insurance or weather insurance could be useful for exhibitions or show organizers, or agribusiness.

Swaps are private contracts struck between market participants. A swap is an agreement to exchange the cash flows of two different securities - Bank A holds bond X, and Bank B holds bond Z, but they agree to swap the coupons. Like forwards or futures, swaps are binding commitments. There is no upfront fee - swaps are priced so that the net present value of both 'legs' is identical when they begin, and exposures are netted out so that only the 'loser' pays.

Conclusion

Risk management is not about avoiding risk. It's not about second-guessing. If you have a bright idea, and carry it out a bit tentatively, because you're afraid it might fail, that's not risk management. If you want to invest in a market but then halve your position amount because you're not all that confident, that's not risk management.

Risk management is thinking through the risks, managing them, selecting the exact risks you want to take, and transferring the other - and then going full steam ahead with your project.

Imagine you're climbing Everest and you come to a crevasse. If you start dodging around and put a toe up to the edge very tentatively, you'll end up falling in. The proper risk manager looks at the risk (falling in the crevasse) and the reward (summiting Everest), and decides to mitigate the risk by throwing a rigid ladder across the crevasse and roping up to a Sherpa at the front and her climbing partner behind.

Risk management isn't once and for all. Risk management needs to be done every single day. It needs a framework for monitoring and controlling risk, and processes that get everyone in the organization to contribute to risk control. And you need to keep your eye open for new risks. What about Brexit - a huge risk that most fund managers and banks hadn't adjusted for?

Let's leave you with one thought - one phrase that should have you reaching for your risk management tools or looking for the exit.

"It's different this time."

British PM Gordon Brown claimed he'd got rid of boom and bust. It wasn't different that time.

Francis Fukuyama said we'd reached the end of history. It wasn't different that time, either.

No, it's not different this time. It's going to play out in different ways, but you can never assume that credit risk has disappeared or that markets will continue going up or that you have a totally fraud-proof credit scoring system. And that, you know, is why you need risk management - because the one thing we do know for certain is that there will *always* be risk.

Check out this book!

Check out this book!

Check out this book!

Resources / Sources of information

Books

Nassim Taleb's *The Black Swan* describes and discusses extreme events and how to cope with them; *Fooled by Randomness* is also very readable. Taleb's *Dynamic Hedging* is less of a crowd-pleaser; it's a really important financial theory book which you'll need some mathematical concepts to best appreciate.

Edward O. Thorp was the inventor of many quantitative strategies among which the most intriguing was his card-counting system for blackjack and baccarat. His *Beat the Market* is well worth reading.

Eric Falkenstein's *Finding alpha* is very readable and even, at times, funny. He also lays into some of the concepts we've explored in this book, like the Capital Asset Pricing Model. It's a fascinating read, perhaps a book to lie down and re-read in a year or so to get the best out of its insights.

The Institute of Risk Management - www.theirm.org - publishes Enterprise Risk Magazine, and has loads of resources on its website for risk managers within larger organizations, ISO qualifying risk management, and so on.

Major consulting firms publish regularly on banking risk management.   McKinsey (**https://www.mckinsey.com/business-functions/risk/our-insights/the-future-of-bank-risk-management**)   and   Deloitte (**https://www2.deloitte.com/.../Banking/lu_inside_issu**

e14_strategic_risk_management.pdf) have particularly interesting approaches.

Finally, the Bank for International Settlements has chapter and verse on banking regulations such as Basel 3. (https://www.bis.org/about/index.htm)

www.ingramcontent.com/pod-product-compliance
Lightning Source LLC
Chambersburg PA
CBHW070130240526
45468CB00002BA/738